Complines

The service of Compline is used in the Northumbria Community as an optional extra to the Daily Office - an ideal way to end the day. Many use it on a regular basis, usually just before retiring to bed. On retreats it can be used to bring time together to a close as the whole household goes into quiet until next morning. These prayers are not lengthy and can be offered in just a few minutes.

It is recommended that a time of quietness should precede Compline, emptying out all the tensions and concerns of the past day and shifting the focus of our attention back to God. Then the sign of the cross can be made silently before starting the spoken prayers.

If you have young children, Compline can be used as bedtime prayers with them or over them, substituting the child's or children's names in the boxed sections whenever they cannot say the prayer for themselves. For example 'In peace will Martha lie down, for it is You, O Lord, You alone who makes her to rest secure.'

There is a different form of Compline for each day of the week. Each is named after an individual from the era of the Celtic Saints, serving as another reminder of the example set by 'good ones of old' who inspire us to seek God as they did. Complines are often said by candlelight – hence the large print used in this booklet.

+ indicates where you might make the sign of the cross

* indicates a change of reader

All say together the sections in **bold type**

The sections between lines should be said by each person in turn

---

SUNDAY – The Ita Compline

+ (silently)

The Sacred Three
to save
to shield
to surround
the hearth
the home
this night
and every night.

* Search me, O God, and know my heart.
  Test me and know my thoughts.

* See if there is any wicked way in me
  and lead me in the way everlasting.

O Father, O Son, O Holy Spirit,
forgive me my sins.
O only-begotten Son of the heavenly Father,
forgive.
O God who is one,
O God who is true,
O God who is first,
O God who is one substance,
O God only mighty,
in three Persons, truly merciful,
forgive.

* O God of life, this night,
  O darken not to me Thy light.

* O God of life, this night,
  close not Thy gladness to my sight.

* Keep Your people, Lord,
  in the arms of Your embrace.
  Shelter them under Your wings.

* Be their light in darkness.
  Be their hope in distress.
  Be their calm in anxiety.

* Be strength in their weakness.

* Be their comfort in pain.

* Be their song in the night.

---

*In peace will I lie down, for it is You, O Lord,
You alone who makes me to rest secure.*

---

* Be it on Your own beloved arm,
  O God of grace, that I in peace shall awake.

**Be the peace of the Spirit mine this night.
Be the peace of the Son mine this night.
Be the peace of the Father mine this night.
The peace of all peace be mine this night
+ in the name of the Father,
and of the Son,
and of the Holy Spirit. Amen.**

MONDAY – The Aidan Compline

+ (silently)

* O Christ, Son of the living God,
  may Your holy angels guard our sleep,
  may they watch over us as we rest
  and hover around our beds.

* Let them reveal to us in our dreams
  visions of Your glorious truth,
  O High Prince of the universe,
  O High Priest of the mysteries.

* May no dreams disturb our rest
  and no nightmares darken our dreams.
  May no fears or worries delay
  our willing, prompt repose.

* May the virtue of our daily work
  hallow our nightly prayers.
  May our sleep be deep and soft
  so our work be fresh and hard.

  **I will lie down and sleep in peace
  for You alone, Lord,
  make me dwell in safety.**

  ---

  *My dear ones, O God, bless Thou and keep,
  in every place where they are.*

  ---

* Into Your hands I commit my spirit;
    I give it to You with all the love of my heart.

* How precious to me are Your thoughts, O God!
    How vast is the sum of them!
    Were I to count them,
    they would outnumber the grains of sand.
    When I awake,
    I am still with You.

I make the cross of Christ
upon my breast,
+ **over the tablet of my hard heart,**
and I beseech the
Living God of the universe –
may the Light of Lights come
to my dark heart from Thy place;
may the Spirit's wisdom come
to my heart's tablet
from my Saviour.

* Christ without sin,
    Christ of wounds,
    I am placing my soul and my body
    under Thy guarding this night,
    Christ of the poor,
    Christ of tears.
    Thy cross be my shielding this night,
    O Thou Son of tears, of the wounds,
    of the piercing.

I am going now into the sleep:
O be it in Thy dear arm's keep,
O God of grace, that I shall awake.

* My Christ!
  my Christ!
  my shield,
  my encircler,
  each day, each night,
  each light,
  each dark.

* My Christ!
  my Christ!
  my shield,
  my encircler,
  each day, each night,
  each light, each dark.
  Be near me,
  uphold me,
  my treasure,
  my triumph.

Circle me, Lord,
keep protection near
and danger afar.

---

* Circle me, Lord,
  keep light near
  and darkness afar.

* Circle me, Lord,
keep peace within;
keep evil out.

The peace of all peace
be mine this night
\+ **in the name of the Father,**
and of the Son,
and of the Holy Spirit. Amen.

TUESDAY
– The Cuthbert Compline

+ (silently)

* I will lie down and sleep in peace
for You alone, Lord,
make me dwell in safety.

**O God, and Spirit, and Jesu,
the Three,
from the crown of my head,
O Trinity,
to the soles of my feet
mine offering be.
Come I unto Thee, O Jesu, my King –
O Jesu, do Thou be my sheltering.**

---

*My dear ones, O God, bless Thou and keep,
in every place where they are.*

---

* Whoever has chosen
to make the shelter of
the Most High
their dwelling place
will stay in His over-shadowing.

* He alone is my refuge, my place of safety;
He is my God, and I am trusting Him.

*   He will rescue you
    from the traps laid for your feet,
    and save you
    from the destroying curse.

*   His faithful promises are your armour.
    You need no longer be afraid
    of any terror by night,
    or the death-arrow that flies by day.

*   The Lord Himself is your refuge;
    you have made the Most High
    your stronghold.

*   Be my strong rock,
    a castle to keep me safe,
    for You are my crag and my stronghold.

*   How precious to me
    are Your thoughts, O God!
    How vast is the sum of them!
    Were I to count them,
    they would outnumber the grains of sand.
    When I awake,
    I am still with You.

---

*I will not lie down tonight with sin, nor shall sin
nor sin's shadow lie down with me.*

O God of life, this night,
O darken not to me Thy light.
O God of life, this night,
close not Thy gladness to my sight.
O God of life, this night,
Thy door to me, O shut not tight,
O God of life, this night.

* Be it on Thine own beloved arm,
O God of grace,
that I in peace shall waken.

(Hymn for optional use)

As the bridegroom to his chosen,
as the king unto his realm,
as the keep unto the castle,
as the pilot to the helm,
so, Lord, art Thou to me.

As the fountain in the garden,
as the candle in the dark,
as the treasure in the coffer,
as the manna in the ark,
so, Lord, art Thou to me.

As the music at the banquet,
as the stamp unto the seal,
as the medicine to the fainting,
as the wine-cup at the meal,
so, Lord, art Thou to me.

As the ruby in the setting,
as the honey in the comb,
as the light within the lantern,
as the father in the home,
so, Lord, art Thou to me.

As the sunshine in the heavens,
as the image in the glass,
as the fruit unto the fig-tree,
as the dew unto the grass,
so, Lord, art Thou to me.

* Jesu, Son of Mary!
my helper, my encircler.
Jesu, Son of David!
my strength everlasting.
Jesu, Son of Mary!
my helper, my encircler.

The peace of all peace
be mine this night
+ **in the name of the Father,**
  and of the Son,
  and of the Holy Spirit.
Amen.

WEDNESDAY
– The Felgild Compline

+ (silently)

**Calm me, O Lord, as You stilled the storm.
Still me, O Lord, keep me from harm.
Let all the tumult within me cease.
Enfold me, Lord, in Your peace.**

* Father, bless the work that is done,
and the work that is to be.

* Father, bless the servant that I am,
and the servant that I will be.

_____

*Thou Lord and God of power,
shield and sustain me this night.*

_____

**I will lie down this night with God,
and God will lie down with me;
I will lie down this night with Christ,
and Christ will lie down with me;
I will lie down this night with the Spirit,
and the Spirit will lie down with me;
God and Christ and the Spirit,
be lying down with me.**

* The peace of God
  be over me to shelter me,

* under me to uphold me,

* about me to protect me,

* behind me to direct me,

* ever with me to save me.

**The peace of all peace
be mine this night**
+ **in the name of the Father,
and of the Son,
and of the Holy Spirit.
Amen.**

THURSDAY
– The Ebba Compline

+ (silently)

* Find rest, O my soul, in God alone:
  my hope comes from Him.

  **Come I this night to the Father,
  come I this night to the Son,
  come I to the Holy Spirit powerful:
  come I this night to God.
  Come I this night with Christ,
  come I with the Spirit of kindness.
  Come I to Thee, Jesus.
  Jesus, shelter me.**

* I will lie down and sleep.
  I wake again,
  because the Lord sustains me.

* By day the Lord directs His love;
  at night His song is with me –
  a prayer to the God of my life.

* Be strong and take heart,
  all you who hope in the Lord.

* This dwelling, O God, by Thee be blest;
  and each one who here this night does rest.

* May God be in my sleep;
   may Christ be in my dreams.
   May the Spirit be in my repose,
   in my thoughts, in my heart.
   In my soul always
   may the Sacred Three dwell.

---

*May the Father of heaven
have care of my soul,
His loving arm about my body,
through each slumber
and sleep of my life.*

**The Son of God be shielding me from harm,
the Son of God be shielding me from ill,
the Son of God be shielding me with power.
The Son of God be shielding me this night.**

* Sleep, O sleep in the calm of each calm.
   Sleep, O sleep in the guidance of all guidance.
   Sleep, O sleep in the love of all loves.
   Sleep, O beloved, in the Lord of life.
   Sleep, O beloved, in the God of life.

**The peace of all peace
be mine this night
+ in the name of the Father,
and of the Son,
and of the Holy Spirit.
Amen.**

FRIDAY – The Boisil Compline

+ (silently)

* O Lord, You will keep us safe
and protect us forever.

**I am placing my soul and my body
in Thy safe keeping this night, O God,
in Thy safe keeping, O Jesus Christ,
in Thy safe keeping, O Spirit of perfect truth.
The Three who would defend my cause
be keeping me this night from harm.**

* I call on You, O God,
for You will answer me;
give ear to me and hear my prayer.

* Show the wonder of Your great love,
You who save by Your right hand
those who take refuge in You from their foes.

* Keep me as the apple of Your eye;
hide me in the shadow of Your wings.

_____

*Lighten my darkness, Lord.
Let the light of Your presence
dispel the shadows of night.*

_____

* Christ with me sleeping,
  Christ with me waking,
  Christ with me watching,
  each day and each night.

* Save us, Lord, while we are awake,
  guard us while we are asleep;
  that, awake, we may watch with Christ,
  and, asleep, may rest in His peace.

**God with me protecting,
the Lord with me directing,
the Spirit with me strengthening
for ever and for evermore.**

* In the name of the Father precious,
  and of the Spirit of healing balm.
  In the name of the Lord Jesus,
  I lay me down to rest.

**The peace of all peace
be mine this night
+ in the name of the Father,
and of the Son,
and of the Holy Spirit.
Amen.**

SATURDAY
– The Patrick Compline

+ (silently)

**In the name of the King of life;
in the name of the Christ of love;
in the name of the Holy Spirit:
the Triune of my strength.**

* I love you, O Lord my strength.
The Lord is my rock,
my fortress and my deliverer.
My God is my rock
in whom I take refuge.

* I will praise the Lord who counsels me;
even at night my heart instructs me.

* I have set the Lord always before me.
Because He is at my right hand,
I shall not be shaken.

---

*I am placing my soul and my body
under Thy guarding this night, O Christ.
May Thy cross this night be shielding me.*

---

* Into Your hands I commit my spirit;
redeem me, O Lord, the God of Truth.

* The God of life with guarding hold you;
  the loving Christ with guarding fold you;
  the Holy Spirit, guarding, mould you;
  each night of life to aid, enfold you;
  each day and night of life uphold you.

**May God shield me;
may God fill me;
may God keep me;
may God watch me;
may God bring me this night
to the nearness of his love.**

* The peace of the Father of joy,
  the peace of the Christ of hope,
  the peace of the Spirit of grace,

**the peace of all peace
be mine this night
+ in the Name of the Father,
and of the Son,
and of the Holy Spirit.
Amen.**

Acknowledgements

The Aidan Compline

'Circle me Lord': from The Edge of Glory by David Adam, SPCK, London.

The Felgild Compline

'Calm me, O Lord': from Borderlands by David Adam, SPCK, London

The Cuthbert Compline

'As the Bridegroom to his chosen': 'Belonging' by John Taule and Emma Frances Bevan, Hymns Ancient and Modern.

Complines

This booklet contains the Complines from the Northumbria Community. The service of Compline is used by many in Northumbria Community as an optional extra to the Daily Office and an ideal way to end the day.

More extensive forms of liturgy, prayers and meditations and daily readings from the Northumbria Community can be found in Celtic Daily Prayer (ISBN 9780007199075) published by Collins and available by mail order from our website **www.northumbriacommunity.org/community-resources-and-shop**

For more information about the Northumbria Community, please contact:

office@northumbriacommunity.org

or visit **www.northumbriacommunity.org**

**Northumbria Community
Nether Springs, Croft Cottage
Acton Home Farm, Felton
Northumberland, NE65 9NU**

call **01670 787645**

ISBN: 978-1-907289-26-2
© Northumbria Community Trust
Registered Charity Number: 1156630

COMMUNITY

9 781907 289262